A YEAR WITHOUT MAKE-UP

Tales of a 20-Something Traveler

STEPHANIE YODER

Thought Catalog Books
Brooklyn, NY

THOUGHT CATALOG BOOKS

Copyright © 2015 by Stephanie Yoder

All rights reserved. Published by Thought Catalog Books, a division of The Thought & Expression Co., Williamsburg, Brooklyn. For general information and submissions: manuscripts@thoughtcatalog.com.

First edition, 2015.
ISBN 978-1517493349
10 9 8 7 6 5 4 3 2 1

Founded in 2010, Thought Catalog is a website and imprint dedicated to your ideas and stories. We publish fiction and non-fiction from emerging and established writers across all genres.

Cover photography by Tiago Aguiar

For Michael, who always believes in me

CONTENTS

ABOUT THIS BOOK

The first thing you should know about me is that I'm a girl who can't sit still.

I love to travel. I love getting lost in a new city, the unfamiliar smells, the history, the people-watching while sitting at a cafe with a drink. I love local beer. I love food: the more unfamiliar the better, although I'll never say no to authentic pizza or tacos. I love wearing the same raggedy pair of flip flops for months on end until they basically disintegrate. I love pushing myself, even when I'm terrified, and I love discovering new things about myself and the world.

Nowadays I'm one of those fortunate yet underpaid individuals who gets to make a living writing about travel, but this wasn't always the case. I used to have a water cooler, a desk and a morning commute just like everyone else. I worked during the week, partied on U Street on the weekends and mostly tried to ignore the fact that I had no idea what I wanted to do next. Maybe I would go to grad school, or change careers, or just put my head down and keep progressing at my boring but inoffensive job.

Instead, I decided to travel. It was the one thing I knew I loved and that had made me happy in the past. I mean, why not? I was young, unattached, unchained. I didn't want to wait until I was old; I wanted to experience the world while I had the energy and wonder to fully appreciate it. One year of backpacking around the world, that would sort me out. Maybe after a year I would be ready to settle down and start a real career.

The second thing to know is that even though I quit my job to go travel, it wasn't an impulsive move. I spent two years mulling my options, saving up money and reading Lonely Planet Thailand before I gave my notice. I decided to start my trip in Japan, where I had a friend teaching English. From there I planned to head to New Zealand, Australia, South East Asia and then towards the Middle East and Europe.

(Spoiler Alert: I didn't make it all the way around the world. Still haven't. I did however spend 9 months in Asia and Australia, learn a lot and meet the love of my life, so it wasn't exactly a wasted trip. More on this later.)

I also started writing about my preparations and later about my adventures on a website, that I titled Twenty-Something Travel. Shockingly, some people out there felt this was worth reading and it led me towards a whole new unexpected career path. But that's not why I started writing, this is why:

I think that in the United States we have a very myopic view of work and leisure. Unlike other cultures where gap years are common (see: the UK and Australia), in the US we are taught from an early age that we need to focus almost exclusively on our education and career. Travel is a luxury that many people simply don't have time for. I think that's bullshit.

There's not really any difference between you and me. I'm not rich, nor am I exceptionally brave (I'm afraid to order pizza on the phone). I'm not crazy. I'm not even that impulsive. I just saw something I wanted more than anything else, so I went after it.

What I found, and how it changed me, is the subject of this quick little book. I culled through hundreds of blog posts about my travel experiences and pulled some of the most essential, then rewrote them almost completely, because I'm a revision addict. What I hope to present is the joy and the misery of travel, as well as the lessons it provides. If it convinces anyone else to take a little time off and see the world, my job will be more than done.

The most important thing for you to know is that you could easily do what I did if you really wanted to. Maybe you don't and that's cool, I still hope you enjoy my story. Maybe you do want to make a life change, and I hope you'll find some useful information in here as well. Hopefully either way, you'll see that there's a huge world out there waiting for you, if you want it.

THE MANIFESTO

So, I started a website, and to kick things off in grand self-help/motivational fashion, I wrote a manifesto. I'd never written a manifesto before, but I had watched *Jerry Maguire* a dozen times, so I felt like I had a handle on the idea.

Here's what I wrote:

You've probably heard it once and over again: Your twenties are supposed to be the best years of your life. This may or may not be true but what is certain is that the experiences you have in the years between 20 and 29 years old are probably going to be some of the most joyous, depressing, scary, confusing and exciting things you will ever have.

Which is what makes now the ideal time to see the world. Some people will tell you to wait to travel until after you are established. Wait until you are making more money. Wait until you are retired. But just when is that perfect time actually going to arrive? Chances are that never again in your life will you have the resources, lack of commitments, energy and good health that you (hopefully) have right now.

You don't need a ton of money.
You don't need to speak a foreign language.
You don't need any special skills.

All you need is a little courage and some serious determination.

There will always be a million reasons not to go. You can always find an excuse. Ignore them. Your friends won't change while you are gone. Your career will still be waiting when you get back.

You can pursue higher education later. You will already be getting one of the greatest educations you can give yourself by seeing the world.

It can be daunting but there is no better time than now.

So go!

CHAPTER 1.

HOW TO SAVE $20,000 AND QUIT YOUR JOB

Rosy manifestos aside, the real thing everyone wants to know is: how do you actually do it? How do you move from an abstract idea to actually waking up in a foreign country?

I saved twenty thousand dollars in two years, ten thousand of that within an eight month period before my trip. As a result, I've become a little bit of an expert on how to save a lot of money quickly. If I pulled this off, you probably can too. I'm not a money genius. Even now I struggle to keep a budget on a monthly basis. I did have determination though, and that gave me discipline.

In a lot of ways, saving money to travel is like going on a diet. When you want to lose weight, you have to change your habits, your intake and output, and you have to adjust the way you think about food. There are a million fad diets but we all know that in reality the only way to lose weight is through healthy diet and exercise.

Similarly, the only way to save a lot of money fast without going insane or giving up is to spend less and make more. It's not glamorous, and it's kind of hard but it gets the job done.

So instead of some elaborate system, here is the common sense way to save money and still see a movie or have a cocktail once in a while:

Set a Goal

When I made the concrete decision to travel I set myself a goal of saving $10,000 in 8 months. I already had $10K in savings and I figured I'd need around $20,000 for what I wanted to do. That meant coming up with an extra $1250 dollars a month, which wouldn't be easy but it was something I felt was achievable based on my situation.

So the first thing you should do, right now, is set yourself a goal. Think about how much money you need to make your dream a reality and how much you can realistically save per month while still being able to like, eat and stuff. You can also set yourself smaller monthly goals to keep up momentum.

It's important when you do this that you don't set yourself up to fail. You have to believe that the goal is obtainable, otherwise the whole thing is still in fantasy territory. Set yourself a minimum amount, then view anything more than that as gravy.

A *word on debt:*

Debt is the worst! I get many, many emails from people who want to travel, but feel trapped by their loan payments.

I don't think that student loans should necessarily prevent you from traveling. It may make things a little tougher and slower, but loans can be worked around. It's something you will need to take into account as you plan your budget and your goals. Personally I had, and still have, student loans that I pay off every month.

When you plan your travel budget, be sure to account for paying your loans (trust me, you do not want to default while you're on the road). Consolidate if you can so that you are only dealing with one monthly payment, and make it religiously, even as you're traveling.

If it's not just student loans we're talking about, if you are deep in credit card debt or home payments or something, then the first step is to get your financial house in order as best you can before planning out your trip. Kind of a bummer, but once you straighten out your finances you'll be good to go.

Cut Back Spending

After you've set your goals it's time for the hard part. Look at where your money is going and figure out where you can cut way back. You will find most of your new savings come from turning off your spending on things you don't really need.

For me, this meant moving in with my mother to save on rent. If you can do this, I highly recommend it — nothing saved me more money as rent is usually a major expense. It wasn't always ideal but I kept my sanity. Even if you can't crash with parents or a relative, downgrading to a smaller apartment or taking on roommates are both options for paying less rent.

It also meant giving up on a lot of poor spending habits. I stopped buying lunch at work and started bringing a bagged one. I gave up online shopping — the amount of money I'd spent on impulse while bored at work was out of control. I started passing up on social opportunities that cost a lot of money: concerts, fancy dinners or clubs, and concentrated on things like hanging out in dive bars.

I didn't strip my life to total austerity because I don't believe that will work. To go back to my diet analogy: if you completely starve yourself you're just going to end up binging later on. I still spent money, but I was much more conscientious about where it was going: only to things that truly mattered to me.

Boost Your Income

It wasn't enough for me to just cut my spending way back, I also needed to get more money coming in. After all, I was only making 37K a year *before* taxes and there's only so much you can squeeze out of that.

So I started looking around for other ways to make a few bucks. The biggest boost to my savings came when I sold my car. I loved my sleek black Jetta but it wouldn't do me much good while I was tromping around Asia. Many people take it even farther than that and offload all the stuff that they won't need in their new life. Honestly I was a bit lazy on this front, but you can make a surprising amount of money selling your old clothes, books and electronics.

I also had money coming in from the blog which, while not a lot, was a helpful extra boost. Most people probably don't have a profitable website but you can still pick up an extra part time job. If you don't have time for that look for smaller opportunities — babysitting, helping someone move, whatever little gigs you can pick up.

Every extra dollar brings you one step closer to your goal, so get creative!

Stay Motivated

It's hard. Living simply for many, many months while everyone you know is continuing to be normal can really get to you.

Keeping your eye on the prize, reminding yourself constantly what you're working for can help a lot. Every $20 I managed to save was a day in South East Asia. Every extra $100 that came in was some cool activity I would get to do somewhere. It's delayed gratification but it works.

Make yourself a separate savings account and don't touch anything that goes in. The highlight of my month used to be depositing a huge chunk of my paycheck into that account. Watching the number jump higher and higher was a reward in and of itself.

Finally, don't be afraid to splurge a little once in a while. During my time of intensive saving I still found the money to fly cross-country to visit a friend in San Francisco. I felt like if I didn't my restlessness would make me lose my mind. Spend money on things that really matter to you and you won't spend it on crap that doesn't.

So to sum up:

Set reasonable goals

Cut back on major expenses

Don't buy crap

Make extra money however you can

Get a separate savings account

Keep your eye on the prize

That's pretty much it. There's a pretty good chance that once you make these changes, you won't ever go back to your old ways. Even now I don't spend money on stupid clothing I don't need or Starbucks coffee. It just doesn't seem worth it anymore. I will however shell out for a plane ticket at a moment's notice.

CHAPTER 2.

DO THE THING THAT SCARES YOU

As I saved my pennies, picked out a backpack and gave notice at my job, I was plagued by a recurring question. Why did it seem like I was the only one doing this?

Over and over people would say, "I wish I could do that!" Perplexed, I always told them that of course they could, if they wanted to.

A lot of it is priorities, but I think another huge barrier for many people, is fear. There are a lot of misconceptions and fears surrounding long-term travel. Among them:

Fear of being unsafe

Fear of being lonely

Fear of missing out on life at home

Fear of deviating from the status quo

And maybe the biggest of all:

Fear of the unknown.

My original plan for this chapter was to go through these one by one pointing out the logical reasons that these fears ring hollow. It wouldn't matter though, because fear is not a rational emotion. I have these anxieties from time to time and I have traveled enough to know the truths behind them. Instead, I want to point out something about these boogie monsters that I think a lot of people don't really think about:

Fear can be a good thing.

Or rather, overcoming your fears can be a really good, healthy thing. Looking fear straight in the eye, taking a deep breath, and forging ahead anyways. It's certainly not an easy or particularly fun experience, but it's on of the most important skills you can learn.

It is important because even back in our regular lives we often have to do things that are scary. Things like first dates, or job interviews, or having babies, or really any major life change at all. If we played it safe all the time nothing would ever happen to us.

Buying that expensive one-way plane ticket to Tokyo was absolutely terrifying. For several hours my fingers hovered over my mouse, daring myself to click the "purchase" button. When I finally hit it I felt this unbelievable surge of relief! That is, until I realized that this meant I actually had to go.

Now, I'm not advocating that you do things that are irrational or dangerous. There is a big difference between playing Russian roulette and learning to scuba dive even though you are afraid of fish. There is a difference between defying your fears and defying common sense, and I think if you can stay connected with the logical part of your brain it's easy to differentiate between the two.

It's about learning to trust yourself. It gets easier as you go. The first time you strike up a conversation with random people at a hostel you may be secretly petrified, but each time you get a little bit bolder. Suddenly you are the chatty friend who talks to random people at bars and nobody believes you when you tell them you are secretly an introvert.

In the days leading up to my departure I often felt paralyzed by the sheer magnitude of what I was doing. Logically I knew it would be amazing, but there were still a million undercurrents of fear in my ocean of excitement.

Then something huge and amazingly unexpected happened. Just two months before my departure I met a boy. A dark, handsome, curly haired boy who had just returned from his own year around the world. A boy who for some unknown reason was really interested in getting to know me.

This was scary in a whole different way. I was supposed to be preparing to leave — mentally and also by you know, shopping for supplies and stuff. Instead I was texting and chatting online late into the night, making impromptu road trips to New Jersey and secretly tumbling head over heels.

Well crap.

That sure wasn't part of the plan.

If he could do the backpack around the world thing though, I'd be damned if I wasn't going to do it too. I would go, and I would force myself to meet people and to encounter situations I had no idea how to handle. I would throw myself out of planes and sleep in dingy hostels and meet random strangers. And I'd come out on the other side the better for it.

CHAPTER 3.

24 HOURS IN TOKYO

So I flew to Tokyo! It was busy and crazy and kind of surreal.

For weeks much of my anxiety had surrounded the first few days of this trip: that jet-lagged time where I didn't have my bearings yet, before I found my travel groove. So I thought I would record a small diary of my first 24 hours off the plane to show exactly how a Round the World trip really gets started. Here is how it all went down:

3:30 PM

Arrive in Tokyo in the middle of a typhoon. After a bumpy 14-hour flight I am exhausted and disoriented. It's 2:30 AM at home. Surprisingly they actually let my strung out looking self through customs (after a photograph and fingerprint check). Can't believe I am in Japan finally.

4:15 PM

I'm always certain that my luggage is going to get lost, but once again I am proven wrong as my purple backpack bounces down the carousel. Together we leave in search of the JR Rail station where I pick up my 14-day Japan Rail Pass. It's one expensive piece of paper, but for the next two weeks it will be my golden ticket to get around Japan.

4:45 PM

Sunny 90 degree Tokyo has apparently been transformed overnight into chilly London. Realize that after all the agonizing packing I still forgot an umbrella. Somehow in my tired haze I manage to get on the correct train and get off at the right station in order to meet my friend Anna. Anna is teaching English in Shizuoka and has come up for the weekend to hang out with me and show me around. As luck would have it she brought an extra umbrella so I won't have to explore Tokyo soaking wet.

6:00 PM

After more walking in the rain with my heavy pack, we arrive at the hotel Anna reserved for us. It's a business hotel: clean and efficient, but somehow internet-less. Like a true tourist, I take pictures of the toilet.

7:30 PM

Head to dinner at a local izakaya (japanese pub). Thankfully all the menus in Tokyo seem to have big pictures on them. I get a big steaming bowl of ramen and struggle to stay awake as we pour over the beat up Lonely Planet Japan someone gave me. I only have two days in the city and there is a LOT to see.

9:00 PM

Back to the hotel to pass out, not a moment too soon.

Sleeeeeeeeeeeeeeeeeeeep

5:30 AM

AWAKE.

Think this may be the only time in my entire life I am ever a morning person. Anna suggests we take advantage of my jet lag and head to the Tsujiki Fish Market which is best viewed early as possible.

6:30 AM

Tsujiki Fish Market. There are more fish here than I could imagine in the entire ocean, much less in Tokyo on a Friday morning. Stall after stall of every kind of fish in Tokyo Bay and beyond. These fish give new meaning to the word "fresh:" some are still flapping their gills and we watch an eel make a frantic leaping bid for escape. It fails and under the knife it goes. We wander the piles of clams, shrimp, octopi and more. Anna is hungry, I am disgusted. Still, I have to admit, it's a pretty awesome sight.

8:00 AM

The row of hole in the wall restaurants lining the streets near the fish bloodbath seem like the perfect place to stop for some sushi. I am not a fish fan, particularly not for breakfast, and generally avoid sushi at all costs, but we're in Japan and it's the first day of the rest of my life. Or whatever. We order a general sampling of tuna, salmon, crab and sea urchin — which is a highly suspicious shade of oozy mustard yellow. This trip is all about doing new things, so gamely I try it all, and it's pretty good! Totally unlike the sushi I've had in America: very, very fresh and smooth — even the sea urchin is tolerable.

9:00 AM

We hop back on the metro and head to Asakusa, a historical area of Tokyo. As soon as I see the red "thunder gates" of Senso-Ji with the enormous hanging lantern, I start to really believe I'm in Japan.

Guarded by some scary looking statue gods, this is the gate for an enormous Buddhist temple, the first of many I'm sure I will encounter. Still a newbie though, I am very impressed and take many pictures of the shiny gates, pagoda and temple. There is a stand where you can get a fortune for 100 yen. Mine tells me (no joke) that this is a good time to start a trip.

This is also my first chance to sample some Japanese sweets from the nearby stalls. Both mochi (a gluey rice ball) and manju (a donut-like cookie filled with red bean paste) are a hit with me. I am too full to even try the ice cream and other delicious items on offer. Soon though...

11:00 AM

Switching back to modern Tokyo, we head over to Ginza, the ritzy shopping neighborhood. I want to experience a famed Japanese department store, so we wander around the very elegant and pricey

Matsuya. I feel like an enormous slob in my gray REI pants and matching gray t-shirt. Guess I will have to get used to that, I didn't exactly pack for style.

The store is 10 stories high with dozens of restaurants and a rooftop garden. My favorite part of the Japanese department stores is the bottom level food court, where many tiny counters sell a huge variety of fancy foods. It may be the jet lag, but I am absolutely stunned by the amount of sweets on display.

2:00 PM

We have been up for nine hours already, and after a quick lunch I am fading fast. Time to head back to the hotel to watch some nonsensical Japanese game shows and take a much needed nap.

A busy first 24 hours abroad, but a good one full of new things, discoveries and delicious food. I really threw myself into everything head first — I was too excited not to. I'm sure not every day will be as frenetic as this one, but if I manage even a quarter as much discovery every day, then this is going to be a mighty fun experience!

CHAPTER 4.

CHINA IS WHAT HAPPENS WHEN YOU'RE MAKING OTHER PLANS

A few years ago, when I was single and at an, erm, a speed dating event (I was supporting a friend OKAY?), I met this guy. This was back when I was living at home, planning my Asia trip and weathering an excruciating wait to finally go travel.

This guy, kind of chubby but nerdy and kind looking, was the last in a long line of guys that evening to ask me what I do (workaholic DC's number one conversation starter). I told him I was quitting my job to travel around the world. Instead of the usual weird looks and skepticism, this guy's face lit up.

"I'm going to travel around the world too! I've got my itinerary all mapped out."

"That's awesome!!" I said, totally shocked, "when are you going?"

"As soon as I meet the right girl to go with me."

Something about the schlubby, uninspired look of this guy told me he may have been waiting for a while already. I'm pretty sure he's still out there somewhere waiting for the right lady with the exact same dream as him.

The thing about waiting for the right person to come with you? It's an excuse. It's a reason not to take the steps that you are scared to take. I'm not saying it's wrong to want a travel companion. But there is something kind of wrong about sitting around, waiting for some guy or girl to show up so your life can begin.

When I made the commitment to go travel, I knew I was making a decision to go it alone. "Isn't there someone who wants to go with you?" my mom would ask pleadingly, "one of your friends maybe?" No Mom, nobody I know is crazy enough to take a year away from their careers and backpack around the world. Except me that is.

So I set my sights on what I wanted, ready to ride off into the sunset alone. Truthfully I was quite proud of my independence, even though I was also pretty nervous. That's when fate did that funny/ awful thing where it smacks you upside the head with the exact thing you were NOT looking for.

That is to say, I met a guy. At a blogging even in New York, just two months before I was set to leave on my great big solo statement trip. Oops.

I had big plans, but I am not so set in my ways to not recognize a golden opportunity when it is standing in front of me dangling a plane ticket. A guy who understands, and shares, my passion for travel and philosophy of life. Someone in the throes of his own world exploration. Someone who thinks I'm capable, not irresponsible, and sees my independence as an attractive quality. And the bonus: he's smoking hot. Someone like that does not come along every day.

And when, after a perfect summer, someone that awesome invites you to come visit him while he's teaching English in China, you find a way to make that happen!

So I threw out my plans to go New Zealand (it was too expensive anyways) and applied for a Chinese visa. It had never even occurred to me to visit China before; the giant country seemed so vast and mysterious, so difficult to parse. Did people just VISIT China? Without a guide or anything?

Yeah, it turns out they do. And I did. It wasn't as hard as I expected either. I spent most of my time in Xi'an with Michael but I also visited Beijing and Shanghai alone and had a great time.

So my trip got upended before it even began and changed pretty dramatically. I still traveled solo for much of my 9 months in Asia, but Michael would occasionally join me in places like Thailand and Vietnam. I never made it to the Middle East and Europe, instead heading back in the opposite direction towards South America. All my best laid plans were shattered.

That was okay though, because not only did I spend time with the man that (spoiler alert) I'm going to marry, I learned one of my most valuable travel lessons: It doesn't matter how rigid or type A you are, your plans WILL change. Some things will fall through, while other, greater things, will fall right in your lap.

When it comes to travel that's a guarantee.

CHAPTER 5.

HOW TO LIVE IN CHINA AS A FOREIGNER

Let's say you unexpectedly move to China. I know that's kind of far-fetched but that's what makes it unexpected right? I won't go into the circumstances that lead me, a clueless white girl who is STILL struggling to learn Spanish after like 10 years, to end up living on a college campus in Xi'an, China (okay, it was a boy, it's always a boy) but basically I was totally shocked by my own circumstances.

So, you find yourself similarly transported to China. To say that you may experience some culture shock is a massive understatement. In my estimation moving to China, particularly anywhere outside of cosmopolitan Shanghai or Beijing, is akin to moving to another planet. All of a sudden every day things become totally incomprehensible: just going to the grocery store or the bank becomes a massive adventure.

I think everybody's China adventure is a little different, but here's a starter course on what you can expect when you make your home on the metaphorical moon.

You will be a celebrity. China is not really known for its ethnic diversity (my city of nine million was 99.97% Han Chinese). If you resemble anything besides a native Chinese person, get ready to stand out like an ostrich walking down the street. If you happen to be pale with blonde hair like myself, the distinction is even greater.

People are going to take your picture. At first you may not notice it because they can be pretty sneaky, but once you catch on it's hard to miss. You will be ambushed by shy teenage paparazzi. The brave ones may even ask to pose with you. Once a family asked me to hold their baby for a portrait. What are they doing with these pictures? I never really found out.

You will have to answer a lot of questions. As you might have guessed, people are really curious about foreigners, so be prepared to give your very important opinion on just about anything under the sun. A sampling:

- Does everyone in the US have a gun?

- Do all Americans have tattoos?

- Have you ever been to Disney World?

- Is America just like on Friends?

- Why aren't you married?

- When are you getting married?

- Really, can you just get married already?

Your lungs will hate you. If you decide to live in a big city, or down-wind of a big city, kiss the ability to take full breaths goodbye. The air quality in China is as bad as you've heard — maybe worse. You know when it's really foggy outside and you can't see five feet in front of you? This is common on a bad air day in China, except it's not fog, it's poison. So since breathing is kind of an essential process, you'll just have to give in to the inevitable shortening of your life-span. If you're anything like me you'll develop a suspicious cancerous sounding cough for months that magically disappears almost immediately after you leave the country.

In China, you are already an old maid. If you are over the age of 24 and unmarried by choice, you do not make sense in China. Even though the women there are smart, beautiful and well-educated, the most important goal for many of them is to land a guy and have a smart, beautiful Chinese baby. My (fairly new, like less than a year) boyfriend and I were the subject of many pointed looks and questions about exactly when and where we would be tying the knot ("Do it here!" one student breathlessly exclaimed, another suggested their home in Inner Mongolia).

Once, in a fit of culture-blindness, I told a group of students that we weren't getting married because we were still too young. At 26. They just shook their heads like "what's that silly blonde ostrich saying now?"

Chinese food is even better than you can imagine. Everyone loves take-out Chinese food, but the stuff you get at home barely even resembles the real stuff. Legit Chinese food is fresh and diverse and even though you won't know what 90% of it is it won't stop you from stuffing it in your face as fast as your chopsticks can move. Seriously, I have traveled all over the world and nothing on earth even compares to the deliciousness of real Chinese food. I don't know how they do it but Chinese chefs can make a plain plate of cucumbers taste like a delicacy.

Also, there are thousands of different dishes to try, and eating out is exponentially cheaper than trying to cook at home (if your apartment even had a kitchen, which it doesn't).

By the way, you can't be a vegetarian in China. I mean I guess you could if you spoke Chinese, but good luck trying to explain yourself when literally everything is fried in pig fat.

You will have to adjust your standards of cleanliness. I'm going to tell you a true story that will probably make you want to die: one day my boyfriend and I were eating at a restaurant when a very sickly looking waiter leaned over and vomited all over the floor. That's not the gross part yet guys, after he finished getting sick everywhere, he grabbed a mop, mopped it up and WENT BACK TO WORK. Nobody in the restaurant batted an eye and after a while, neither did I. It's just kind of the way things are, and it's better to just not think about it.

This doesn't just apply to the food either. In my town, public trash cans were not a thing that existed, people just threw their rubbish into the nearest bush or gutter. And the spitting — I still hear the spitting sometimes, in my nightmares.

Things are not going to make sense, accept it. There are so many things about China that I never figured out: why do the ATMs only give out 100 RMB notes when nobody will cash more than a 20? Why don't they refrigerate milk? If Chinese babies don't wear diapers, how do parents keep from getting surprise pooped on every day?

Eventually you just have to embrace the chaos. Embrace the congestion and the bad air quality and embrace the guy on the street selling scorpions on a stick (well, maybe not literally). You won't know what's going on but really, it's okay. It's zen.

It's really hard to summarize China in any neat way — it's so enormous and so different and so many things happened that I STILL don't understand. One thing it never is though, is boring.

CHAPTER 6.

THE OLDEST BACKPACKER

Contrary to the chaos you might observe at a party hostel on a Saturday night, backpacking isn't just for the young. I've met all kind of people in common rooms around the world: from brave 18-year-old solo travelers to cool dudes old enough to be my dad.

Or, in the case of Bill, my grandfather.

Finding my hostel in Beijing was kind of a nightmare. It was well past dark and the hostel was down a dark, poorly signposted alley that I walked by about four times before realizing where I needed to go. My stress levels were already high, so when I finally went to claim my bunk and stumbled across a snoring geriatric, I was a little alarmed. I'd been expecting the usual mix of young party kids, frugal couples and other solo twenty-somethings, not dentures in a glass next to the bed. The alarm turned to annoyance as his serious snoring kept me up late into the night.

The next day over complimentary tea and toast I sat down and actually had a chat with my roommate. His name was Bill, he was 74, a navy veteran, and as it turned out, pretty awesome. He's been traveling the world non-stop for six years now. He's been through Europe, the Middle East and much of Asia. He'll travel for six months at a time, then take six weeks off to visit his children and grandchildren in the States before leaving again. He told me that people often call him Grandpa Sunshine because he brings good weather wherever he goes.

So what lessons can we young'uns learn from Grandpa Sunshine?

Exploration is a Part of Human Nature

"The biggest problem with kids today," Bill told me, "is that they've lost the drive to explore. It's human nature to want to see what's out of sight, what's over the next mountain."

Personally I can't agree more: the desire to learn and explore is something innate and important, and I think that many of us (particularly in the

US) neglect those urges. I think that's part of why travel is so dangerously addictive: once you uncover that drive to explore and discover, it's pretty hard to keep denying it.

Life Changes Fast

In one year Bill's life was turned totally upside down: his wife of 30 years died of cancer and his house was destroyed by a hurricane. It was then that he decided to take the insurance money and use it to travel around the world — he's been going ever since.

Nobody wants to experience tragedy, but it's a fact that the twists and turns of life can be radical and sudden. I think that's part of the reason some people embrace travel: it's also constant change and growth. Instead of allowing devastation to take hold, Bill took control of his life and started pursuing the things that really mattered to him.

Ignore the Nonbelievers

Bill's grown-up children think he's lost his mind, "they keep asking when I'm going to just come home." I think that anybody who has traveled long term is familiar with the nagging doubt that comes from the people who just don't get it. They are always going to be there, the key is learning how to manage them effectively while staying true to yourself.

Push Your Limits

Bill's kids weren't the only ones skeptical about his abilities: the Chinese staff in the hostel simply did not know what to do with him — particularly when he insisted he was able-bodied enough to join the rigorous Great Wall hiking tour on offer at reception. Torn between traditional respect for elders and sheer disbelief the staff vigorously tried to dissuade him from hiking even though he insisted he could do it. Bill handled this with grace and firm resistance.

Okay, so you may not be a septuagenarian with something to prove, but it never hurts to push yourself a little. I mean here I was, sitting on the couch like a lazy bum, fretting over how hard the hike might be. It *was* pretty tough. But it was so worth it and I'm glad I pushed myself to do it instead of visiting some pansy part of the wall like Badaling.

STOP Making Excuses

Bill walks with a cane, wears thick glasses and has dentures. After many years of traveling he's on a pretty tight budget so he travels slowly and sleeps in dormitories. Still, he loves traveling and has no plans to stop anytime soon.

If that guy can keep it up, so can you. I mean come on guys.

When I last saw Bill he was sitting in the sun, typing on his ENORMOUS Dell laptop. Grandpa Sunshine. It certainly is true that my time in Beijing was the clearest and sunniest few days I spent in China. Really though, I think he gets his nickname from how inspiring he is to other travelers. I mean, I hope when I'm in his age I'm still doing the things I love, whether that is still backpacking or something else entirely.

CHAPTER 7.

HOW TO HAVE THE WORST DAY EVER IN PHUKET (AND HOW TO TURN IT AROUND)

You would think that two travel bloggers traveling together would have everything down to a science, but on our first trip together, Mike and I seemed to be working hard to prove that this is not the case. It seems that no matter how much experience you have, pitfalls, errors and plain dumb luck always throw themselves in your path.

This was particularly true of our first full day of traveling alone together. Having been to Thailand before, Mike told me (correctly) that Phuket is really not that nice of a place and we should minimize our time there. The plan was to spend one day exploring the island via motorbike, spend the night, then head out to Ko Phi Phi in the morning. What followed can only be described as one really rough day:

Steps for a Perfect Bad Day

1. Take an overnight bus from Bangkok to Phuket. Sleep maybe 1/13 of the trip and spend the rest of the night counting headlights in the dark.

2. Arrive in Phuket at the peak of high season with no accommodations. Walk about a kilometer in the searing heat with your bloated backpack slowly cutting off your air supply. Hotels in Phuket are plentiful, but all seem to be entirely booked. Finally find a guesthouse with vacancies and a fair price. Marvel that it's actually pretty nice.

3. Upon arriving in your room, drop your backpack on the floor, shattering a bottle of red wine inside. You bought that wine in Hunter Valley, Australia and lugged it around for an entire month — you were planning to drink it tonight. Watch in disbelief as seemingly endless amounts of wine seep through the entire contents of your pack. Resist the urge to burst into tears as you empty everything you own onto the bathroom floor while Mike frantically mops up the disaster zone.

4. Accidentally lock passports and wallet in a broken, practically impenetrable safe. Force management to come open it.
5. Successfully rent motorbike for just 200 baht. Realize motorbiking is actually super fun in an I-could-smash-my-skull-at-any-moment kind of way. Drive for maybe half an hour — get as far as Patong Beach and promptly be pulled over by a terminally grumpy policeman who demands loudly in Thai to see your driver's license. Realize your boyfriend left his license in the guesthouse for safekeeping. Cop lectures angrily and confiscates bike.
6. Walk a rough kilometer, past scores of prostitution bars and harassing tuk tuk drivers to police station. Watch policeman leisurely eat his lunch before dealing with you. Pay no-license fine of 300 baht ($10). Walk a kilometer back to beach to bail out the motorbike.
7. Bike back to guesthouse to retrieve license and realize that somehow you've again locked it in the impenetrable broken safe. Give up on life.

And how to turn it around:

1. Take a deep breath.

2. Get owner (who now thinks you are a moron) to come unlock the safe. Retrieve license.
3. Get back on the bike. Take a new route this time; a random turn off the main highway that leads you to a street completely absent of tourists and full of local Thai going about their business. It's peaceful here, and interesting.
4. Watch your first Thai sunset over Phrom Thep beach.
5. Stop for dinner at a beautiful restaurant overlooking the harbor. Eat spicy curry and drink out of coconuts.
6. Drink a beer. Realize that your boyfriend and you survived your first absolutely disastrous day of travel together without murdering each other. Think maybe things weren't so bad after all.

CHAPTER 8.

THAILAND IS DISNEY WORLD FOR GROWN UPS

In retrospect maybe my expectations were out of whack. After all, Ko Phi Phi is a tiny island in the Andaman Sea, but it's also a HUGE tourist destination. In my head I pictured white beaches, sparkling water, a coconut in my hand — basically paradise. Instead what I found was a smaller, more backpacker friendly version of Phuket. A place where partying and consumerism far supersede authenticity, and relaxation is almost impossible.

It's illuminating though. I think I'm starting to grasp why Thailand is so hugely popular with tourists. It's not just because it's gorgeous (although it is) or warm or even so cheap. All of those things are great selling points of course, but it's more than that. In Thailand everything is for sale — and cheap. If you've got western dollars to spend it's a fantasy world — it's Disneyland for grown ups. Well, maybe adolescents.

In Thailand you can have anything you want. You can go scuba diving, cliff jumping, you can ride on the back of an elephant or pet a tiger. You can watch women shoot ping-pong balls out of their va-jay-jays (you know, if you want to). And sex: backpacker sex, prostitution, ladyboys, peep shows, you can have pretty much anything if you're willing to pony up the cash and ignore your conscience.

Booze that's cheaper than water, drugs of all varieties, delicious food for cheap cheap cheap. You can party all night long and dance on the beach until dawn. The only payback is your hangover the next day. There seem to be no consequences at all as long as you know how to play the game.

Little Phi Phi is a perfect example of this. Just 50 years ago it was a practically deserted tropical island full of fishermen and not much else. In the 90s its popularity with backpackers began to grow, particularly because of its association with the movie *The Beach*, which was filmed nearby. It was devastated by the 2004 tsunami but has largely bounced back (at least the commercial parts have). The main strip of the island is now jam packed with souvenir shops, internet cafes, bars and guesthouses. You can't walk down the street without noticing a hundred touts and advertisements offering to take you to the famous movie beach.

Now, I've never seen the movie version of *The Beach*, but I've read the book twice. It's an essential backpacker novel. I find it incredibly ironic that the scene on Phi Phi is exactly what Richard, the main character, was trying to escape from. He flees from the chaos of Bangkok's Kho San Road in hopes of finding a quiet, perfect beach. An escape from the travel industry and the pressures that surround it. Now, thousands of backpackers, ostensibly seeking the same thing, have turned what was probably once paradise into a circus.

And, in high season at least, it really is a circus. Once darkness falls the bars start blasting and the drinks start flowing. The girls wander around in various states of undress and the guys hoot and holler. Electric lights blink all around, totally obscuring the stars as thumping beats pound out on a dance floor next to the ocean. It's fun really, quite a sight to see. But after a couple nights the glitz starts to fade and you long for a little peace.

If Ko Phi Phi is Disneyland than Ko Phangan is like some sort of psychedelic war zone. Actually that's not quite right. Only Haad Rin, the southernmost tip of the island is a wild circus party of buckets, bars, flashing lights and fire shows.

The pinnacle of the partying is the monthly Full Moon Party, when the area explodes with drunken twenty-somethings. My guidebook describes the event as "*Apocalypse Now* without the war," and that's pretty damn accurate. At night the beach is alive with thumping bass and battling dancers wearing tribal face paint. The fire dancers and flaming torches that illuminate the sand further enhance the apocalyptic feeling. It's thrilling yes, but also slightly sinister. When the sun comes up the beach is a wasteland of abandoned flip-flops and empty buckets.

And, like a war, there are serious casualties. This tiny town has over 40 medical centers — all catering to injured tourists. Some will be burned playing with fire, others will fall, fight or attempt to go swimming while seriously intoxicated. Another danger: the police, who troll the beaches arresting anyone possessing or attempting to purchase drugs. Still other people end up drugged, robbed or ripped off. It's a treacherous place.

So in Thailand you can have it all — all of the guilty pleasures your heart desires. Some of these things are more ethical than others, it's true. Far be it from me to deny anyone a good time. I've certainly been doing my share of drinking and carousing since I got here. I get the appeal — but there's something about it that's just so... removed from real life. A real problem that's so easy to ignore, until you accidentally stumble down the wrong alley in Phi Phi and discover the run-down, not-yet restored shacks where many of the locals are still living. We may be living in a fantasyland, but not everyone here is.

It's fun to visit Disneyland; to kind of forget that there's a world outside of tonight, and the dancing and the next bucket of cheap Thai rum. But nobody gets to live at Disneyland — and you probably wouldn't like it if you did. It's loud and it's crazy, and ultimately it's fake. In the morning, when the hangover kicks in, all I find myself craving is a really perfect beach.

CHAPTER 9.

THE BACKPACKER MARATHON

Travel, particularly budget travel, isn't all about jet-setting from one glamorous destination to the next. When you have to watch your wallet, getting from one point to the next can be a tedious and time-consuming process. I'll go out on a limb here and say that transportation is many people's least favorite aspect of travel. Short of train rides (and awesome road trips), transportation is actually a major pain in the ass.

Take for example, my journey from Ko Samui, Thailand to Ho Chi Minh City, Vietnam, two cities less than 500 miles apart on the map:

3:00 PM Monday — Leave our fabulous guesthouse in Ko Samui and walk up to the main road where a shuttle bus was supposed to pick us up. It's pouring rain and the bus is late. We stand in the rain for about 45 minutes until the bus finally arrives. It's already packed to the gills with other people so Mike and I squeeze into the front seat with the driver.

4:00 PM — Arrive at the bus depot and play Russian roulette with the bus drivers until we finally find the correct bus. Earlier we had decided on the mid-range (700 baht) option because it was supposed to have more legroom and a bathroom on board. Quickly we realize that our seats in the front row actually give us LESS legroom and that the lights don't work in the bathroom, requiring some balancing magic.

4:30 PM — The bus takes us to a ferryboat (Ko Samui being an island and all) where we are required to offload. The ferry itself is quite massive and it's stopped raining by now, so our two-hour sea journey is not too bad. We feast on pocky, homemade potato chips and cups of noodles.

6:30 PM — Ferry reaches the mainland so we climb back onto the bus. Sometimes these overnight buses show movies (last time we watched *Step Up 3*dubbed in Thai), but tonight all is quiet. Mike and I play Trivial Pursuit on my iPod — we each win two games.

8:30 PM — Stop for dinner — included in the ticket price. It consists of somewhat dodgy looking communal Thai food served at small tables.

9:00 PM — Back onto the bus which, by the way, is colder than my refrigerator at home. WHY DO BUSES DO THIS? Every single night bus I've ever been on, no matter the country, has been hypothermia inducing. Do people enjoy this? The thin pink blanket they hand out is absolutely no match for the unending torrent of freezing air. Huddled together to conserve heat, we watch *The Motorcycle Diaries* on Mike's computer. It's a great movie, but I find myself drifting...

1:00 AM Tuesday — AWAKE. Slowly lull back to sleep then again blasted AWAKE. Driver sure loves his horn. It's a vicious cycle that continues until daybreak, making sure I get little to no useful sleep.

5:00 AM — We arrive in Bangkok and clamor off the bus. Immediately half a dozen taxi drivers pounce on me asking where I want to go. I push them away and try to get my bearings. There's a problem: We have no idea where we are. We'd assumed we'd alight at the Southern Bus Station, since we left from there and we were, you know, coming from the south. Not so — this place is totally unfamiliar and we are stumped. Attempts to ask at the information desk prove fruitless.

5:30 AM — Jump in a taxi towards the airport. Our flight doesn't leave for many, many hours but we figure it's cheapest to go directly there. I hold my breath that this driver will not take us on a "scenic tour" of Bangkok and luckily he doesn't. He must be tired too.

6:15 AM — Arrive at the airport. Our flight doesn't leave until 3:55 PM, which means we've got massive amounts of time to kill. Sleepily eat an overpriced breakfast. Beg the check in lady at Air Asia to let us check in REALLY early but she says no way, we have to come back at 1 PM. Crap.

1:00 PM — At 1 PM on the dot we are at the counter to check our luggage. We are slightly concerned because, due to bad math, we've accidentally overstayed our Thai visa by one day. According to the internet this means we just need to pay 500 baht fine, but we want to get through customs early in case there are any issues.

1:30 PM — Go through customs and security. Things go smoothly — we don't even have to pay the fine. Apparently overstaying by one day is okay — any more is a problem.

2:00 PM — We decide to celebrate our departure by spending our extra baht on absurdly expensive cocktails and sushi. I never remember to change my money after departure so I always try to spend it all before I leave.

3:55 PM — Hop on our flight to Vietnam! It's only an hour and a half so not much chance to catch up on sleep.

5:30 PM — Land in Ho Chi Minh City, excited but exhausted. We bought our Vietnam visas online so we need to jump through a few bureaucratic hoops before we can cross through customs. Our lovely guesthouse has sent someone to pick us up from the airport, which saves us the trouble of trying to navigate the city on our own.

6:30 PM — Finally arrive at our guesthouse. Time to eat and relax after 26 hours of straight travel. And SLEEP.

These kind of endurance travel marathons are pretty typical when your priority is getting somewhere cheaply, not rapidly. Could we have simply flown from Ko Samui to HCMC? Yes, and it would have taken us maybe three hours. But it would have cost us hundreds of dollars more. And that's just not the backpacker way.

CHAPTER 10.

BEING THE BAD GUY

Whenever I am about to visit a new country I make a mental inventory of the things that I associate with that place. When I think of Vietnam I think of: rice paddies, spring rolls and war.

War is probably the biggest thing that most of the western world associates with Vietnam. Although I was born a decade after the end of the Vietnam War, its cultural legacy is still very clear to me. *Miss Saigon*, *Apocalypse Now*, Tim O'Brien and more made the entire situation much more vivid than any history book. My parents can't get over the fact that we now live in a world where their daughter can visit Vietnam as a tourist. "When I was your age," says my Dad, "we were all trying NOT to go to Vietnam."

So even with all the things I think I know about the Vietnam War, I realized that the Vietnamese probably have a very different outlook and attitude on it. For starters I knew that they called it the "American War," which sounds odd but makes a lot of sense. I wanted to know what the Vietnamese attitude was about this terrible time that entangled both of our countries, so one of our first stops in Ho Chi Minh City (formerly Saigon) was the War Remnants Museum.

It was... an awkward visit, to say the least.

The museum, which costs something like 75 cents, is a gray warehouse of a building, with a courtyard filled with re-appropriated American tanks, helicopters and fighter planes. Inside the first focal point plastered on the wall:

We hold these truths to be self-evident, that all men are created equal, that they are endowed by their Creator with certain unalienable Rights, that among these are Life, Liberty and the pursuit of Happiness.

Crucial words from the Declaration of Independence, thoughtfully positioned next to a picture of an American Soldier executing a Viet Cong soldier. Subtly. And a pretty good indicator of what was to come. Image after gory image of dead Vietnamese, dismembered body parts and soldiers terrorizing civilians.

It went on: victims of Agent Orange, dead babies in jars, simulation tiger cages and more. It was weird. And mortifying. And also kind of infuriating. I have absolutely no doubt that the United States did some really horrible things. It was a terrible and ill-advised war. But this place was just too much. What about all the horrible things that the Viet Cong did? Not even mentioned among the debris. I see pictures of locked up Viet Cong, but where is the exhibit on the infamous Hanoi Hilton? War is hell no doubt, but it's a two-sided inferno.

Now, the museum is run by the government, so of course its sole purpose is to booster the party line. In Vietnam, like everywhere else, history is written by the victors. What I was looking at wasn't the actual beliefs of the majority of the people in Vietnam — it was pure propaganda. Once I grasped this, the entire museum experience became less emotional and more academic.

In my travels I've had the opportunity to visit a few different places that have been negatively effects by US actions. I reflected on the bombed out buildings of Belgrade and the atomic bomb site in Hiroshima. The latter is probably more comparable to Vietnam: severe destruction and civilian casualties during wartime. The Peace Park in Hiroshima is almost the polar opposite of this museum though: it's a monument to what was lost, a (fair) explanation of what happened and a plea to make sure it never happens again. I think that ultimately had far more impact on me then the guilt-fest in Saigon.

So what's the difference? Well, the Japanese have had much longer to recover from their wounds. And the Japanese lost the war. America did some really horrible things in both countries, but Japan at least recognizes that we weren't operating in a void. To do that requires a level of self-criticism that the Vietnamese government is clearly not comfortable with.

The good news is, the War Museum is more of a novelty than anything else. It does not represent the views of most people in Vietnam. Things might change when I go up North, but here in the south people are friendly and open. Based on the people I've been lucky enough to meet so far, their opinions on Americans range from indifferent to ecstatic. As one guy told me "That was a long time ago, a lot of bad things happened, but now we must move on."

CHAPTER 11.

A LOVE LETTER TO VIETNAM

If I had a dollar for every time someone has asked me what my favorite place is, I would definitely not have to blog for money anymore. It's such a common question, but it's so hard to answer: are we talking food? Culture? Scenery? The best place to lay on a beach?

I usually give a top three that changes based on my mood, but one country that nearly always makes the list is Vietnam.

People seem to either love or hate Vietnam. I've met many travelers who complained that the country is too dirty, too hectic, too demanding. That the people are greedy and unwelcoming. While there's a grain of truth to these things, that's not the way I saw this country at all.

Traveling here wasn't always easy. There were definitely huge moments of frustration: things like getting lost for the third time before noon, or being forced to wait three hours for a mediocre meal during Tet. There were setbacks like broken cameras and lost ATM cards. There were some truly terrifying night bus rides, strange encounters and moments when I was ready to pack it all in.

Yet, in all of the chaos there were really rewarding moments that made me love travel, love my life, and love Vietnam. Here's why:

The People

More than one person has confided in me that Vietnamese people have been the most unfriendly of all their travels. It's true that up north people are more reserved (unless they want to sell you something), but we met some of the nicest people ever down south. Vietnamese people have beautiful smiles and even when they don't speak English will give you a wave and a greeting. They can be shy, but many love to talk to you with a friendly curiosity.

The little kids are the best though. I never get tired of them waving and shouting hello. Or staring up at me with total puzzlement. Or in the case of one little girl, crying hysterically while her mother laughed and shoved her towards me.

The Food

Holy cow, the food in Vietnam is second only to China in cheapness and deliciousness. After a month in Thailand I was getting pretty tired of eating green curry (no matter how good it is), and luckily in Vietnam there is an almost infinite variety of meals. The cuisine is influenced by Thai, Chinese and French cuisine — basically a trifecta of tasty. I liberally ate from restaurants, street food stalls and even took a Vietnamese cooking course to hopefully reproduce some favorite dishes at home (of course giving my cooking skillz, this isn't very likely). My favorite dishes were fried tofu in tomato sauce, rice pancakes and crispy noodles. Oh and crispy French bread. Can't get enough of that.

Could have passed on the artichoke tea though. Blech.

The Electricity

Vietnam is one of the fastest growing countries in the world, both in terms of population and economy. It has a very young population, which makes the place pretty exciting. Constantly dodging motorbikes drove me nuts, but I loved the feeling of walking down the street and discovering something new each day. From a new street food stand, to a group of kids playing kick the can, to a group of old women drinking beer and gossiping, there was always something going on. The people-watching was unparalleled.

The Beer!

From Saigon Beer in Ho Chi Minh City to Hanoi Beer in, you guessed it, Hanoi, Vietnam had a huge variety of cheap and good beer. Most beers were only popular regionally, so we kept discovering new ones. My favorites were probably Saigon, Huda Beer in Hue and Halida in Hanoi. Best of all was the "fresh beer" in Hoi An that sold for 3000 dong a glass. At 15 cents, that's got to be some of the cheapest beer in the world! Yummy too.

The Weird

From a cow on a motorbike in HCMC to a dinosaur and love-themed amusement park in Dalat, Vietnam was filled with things that just made me go "wha?"

My favorite site in Hanoi was the absolutely bizarre Ho Chi Minh Museum. It's a museum dedicated to the life of the first president of modern Vietnam, portrayed in an elaborate, modern art style. There are giant fruit bowls, cars coming through walls and an abstract representation of the inside of Minh's skull. Very bizarre.

Six weeks was not enough time. Although I was excited to move on to Cambodia and Laos, I wasn't thrilled to be leaving Vietnam. So many places I go I feel like I leave a little piece of my heart behind that I can only hope to someday go back and reclaim.

CHAPTER 12.

HOW TO STAY SAFE TRAVELING SOLO

It's different traveling alone as a girl. I hate that, but it's true.

Over the past year I've traveled in a variety of combinations: as a couple, with a female friend and yes, solo. The three experiences were pretty different, both in terms of how I traveled and how I was treated. Most enlightening was traveling with my boyfriend. As he is also an extensive solo traveler I got to have the unique experience of comparing the ways we travel.

On his last solo trip to South East Asia, Michael had a pretty great time doing things that I, as a solo female, would probably never have attempted. Things like accepting an invitation from a man on the train in Bangkok and spending a week with his family, sleeping on the beach in Ko Phi Phi because he couldn't find a cheap enough hostel room and partying like a (very drunk) rock star in Vang Vieng.

I am a feminist and an egalitarian, but I'm also a realist with a mom who worries a lot. Sleeping alone out in the open or getting piss drunk on my own are just not reasonable or safe things for a woman to do in the world we live in. They're not exactly safe things for a guy to do either, but the threat level is higher for women.

I thought I would try to reassure everyone by providing some simple safety tips that can make all the difference when you are out there on your own. I've tried to come up with some tips that are more useful than "wear a fake wedding ring," and I think all of these tips are applicable to both men, women and people who aren't traveling solo.

Okay, now that is out of the way, here are some simple ways to stay safe on the road:

Watch Your Drink

I love beer as much as the next beer-loving girl, but solo travelers have to be extra careful to keep an eye on their beverage. There have been cases, all over the world, where people have been drugged and robbed, assaulted or worse (this happens to men, too). Don't let your drink out of your sight and be wary of people who offer to buy you drinks.

Taxis

Pay attention to what kind of car you are getting into. If you are concerned, have your guesthouse call a taxi for you. If your bag is in the trunk of the taxi, don't pay the driver until after you've recovered it.

Know Your Surroundings

I love to wander aimlessly in new cities, but at night I try to always know where I'm going and to avoid dark streets or alleyways if I can help it. I also always write down the name and address of my hostel, or grab their business card on my way out the door, just in case I get really lost.

It's Okay to Be a Jerk

Don't worry about manners if you are genuinely feeling unsafe. Women in particular are conditioned to always be polite, even when we feel uncomfortable. Predators know this, and they take advantage of your good nature. But safety always trumps manners. Don't be bullied into giving out information or agreeing to things you're not comfortable with. If someone is making you feel weird, just leave or tell them to get lost. Don't even worry about looking weird or rude.

Look Out for Each Other

Do you believe in karma? I do. And even if I didn't, I believe in being a decent human being, so I always keep an eye out for travelers who might need a helping hand. At hostels I always have my eyes peeled for girls who maybe had too much to drink and need some assistance, or people who look like they need help getting out of an uncomfortable situation. If we all help each other out, then we'll all be better off as a result.

Ultimately, safety on the road (or at home really) is about trusting your instincts and not being afraid to advocate for yourself (like I said, it's OKAY to be a jerk). I recommend that anyone traveling alone check out the book *The Gift of Fear* by Gavin De Becker. While a little paranoia-inducing, there are some really great tips about learning to assess the safety of a situation, and how to listen to your "gut."

That said, I don't believe in living in fear. The world is by and large a safe place, full of amazing things. 98% of the time when I'm traveling I'm absorbed in the culture, the people and the sights, but there's always that 2% of me that feels the need to be vigilant.

I truly believe the world is not an unsafe place and I live my life by that philosophy. I do think though, that the world is a very different place sometimes for men than it is for women, and often times in a detrimental way. Someday that will change, but not until the world learns to recognize the meaning of respect.

CHAPTER 13.

CAMBODIAN CONVERSATIONS PART 1

Phnom Penh, Cambodia:

"That is the fakest 100 dollar bill I have ever seen."

The young man looks up at me expectantly. Behind the innocence in his eyes is a mischievous sparkle. He's handsome, in a boyish way, and he wears the uniform of a front desk clerk. I was sitting, eating my complimentary breakfast baguette in the lobby of the King Guest House when he sat down across from me. He seems totally friendly — except for the fact that he's clearly trying to rip me off.

"You got change?" He asks, casually brandishing a $100 bill. Or at least, what a $100 bill would look like if you photocopied it, then cut around the edges slightly haphazardly. I didn't have the change even for a real bill, but this isn't even a remotely good fake.

"That's fake." I say, with a smile on my face. I'd only gotten to Phnom Penh yesterday but I was already learning the rules of the game. Maybe he was trying to rip me off, but there was no way I was falling for it.

"Okay, then, $20?"

"I'm not giving you any money, that bill is fake — it's too small!"

"$10 then," he says, undeterred. Were we bargaining?

"Look buddy, I'm American. I know what a $100 bill looks like."

He stares at me and when he realizes I'm not budging suddenly his whole demeanor changes. "I'm just joking!" He announces to the room. We are friends now.

His expression turns serious as he starts into what I've come to think of as the "Cambodian interview:"

Where are you from?

How old are you?

Where is your husband?

He seems to find my answers completely unsatisfactory but charges on.

Do you know Tiger Woods?

Eventually his friend sits down at the table as well. He's thumbing through a stack of fake-o hundreds. I ask to see them — they look even worse up close.

"They are too small you see, they need to be bigger," I take out a $1 bill for comparison. Why am I giving this guy forgery tips?

"If I make them bigger you will be able to see they are fakes!" he laughs. Can't really argue with that.

The friend wanders off and before I know it my desk clerk is telling me about his village three hours away. How he's only been in Phnom Penh four months. He hates it, it's too busy, but he likes the money. He thinks maybe he will go to Siem Reap and work there instead; there are lots of guesthouses.

He tells me about India and how he's always wanted to go. He's never been outside of

Cambodia of course, not even to Laos although he tells me it's "nice." India is his dream. There's a particular Buddhist temple far up in the mountains that he longs to visit. He needs to go before he's too old to hike it himself. The people are poor in India, he says, but tourism helps them.

"Like Cambodia."

"I guess," he says, looking uncomfortable. Cambodia may be the poorest country I've ever visited but it's not INDIA poor. Geez.

I have to marvel a bit. One minute this guy is trying to hustle me, the next he's spilling out his life dreams. I've done nothing to deserve such openness besides being willing to listen. Cambodia seems to be the one place in the world where greed and friendship are can completely coincide.

I feel bad that I have to cut our conversation short, but I only have one full day in the city and I need to get a move on. When we stand up he is all business again, eye back on the dollar as he asks me:

"You want tuk tuk?"

CHAPTER 14.

CAMBODIAN CONVERSATIONS PART 2

Sihanoukville, Cambodia:

I am weak.

Before I even sat down in a beach lounger, I'd resolved that I wasn't going to give any money to the touts that roam the beach in Sihanoukville, a resort town on the surprisingly beautiful Cambodian coast. Yet here I was, only an hour later, having my toenails painted pink while I picked out friendship bracelets.

You see, the salespeople are a bit of a nuisance in this part of the world. You can barely get a moments peace between the women and children selling tropical fruits, bracelets, pedicures and massages. In addition to being annoying, it's hard to see small children, sometimes VERY small children, wandering the beach hawking wares. Most of what I've read recommends that you not reward them with money, as it only feeds into the system and keeps the kids out of school and on the beach.

So I was resolved not to pour any money into the surfside economy. Yet, after turning away about a dozen people pleading with me to buy something, anything, I finally succumbed. After watching a very nice and chatty woman conversationally threading the legs of the girl next to me, I found myself agreeing to a $3 pedicure. She was a grown up after all, and trust me, I REALLY needed a pedicure.

"You really need a pedicure." She informed me after examining my grimy feet.

"I know, I haven't had one since I left home six months ago." She looked at me dubiously then whipped out her box of tools and went to work sanding and massaging.

While she was working a little girl, maybe seven years old sat down next to me. She was wearing a blue jumpsuit and carrying an armful of bracelets. She smiles up at me and I shake my head firmly no. But my feet are on lock down so I have no escape from her friendly curiosity.

"Where are you from?" When I tell her the United States her face lights up, "Your flag is red, white and blue, just like the Cambodian flag!"

She's so earnest but already a keen saleswoman I can tell. I'm really curious about what kind of childhood someone like her has, so I start in with the questions.

Do you go to school?

"Yes, in the mornings. I work on the beach in the afternoon."

Where are your parents?

"They work on the beach too. So do my brother and sisters."

Do you like this job?

"Yes, because I get to meet people and practice my English."

Her answers sound a little rehearsed to me, but her smile is definitely genuine. She whips out her threads and starts to knit me a friendship bracelet — free of charge. For the colors she chooses red, white and blue. I have to admit I'm charmed by all of this so I do give in and buy about $5 worth of beach trinkets, before she happily skips away.

"Is that your daughter?" I ask my pedicurist as she files my nails.

She shakes her head with a look I can't quite read. "No. I don't let MY children work. They are in school."

I pick out a light pink nail polish and she explains to me that when her husband left her seven years ago for another woman she had no idea what to do to feed her family. She had four children, no education and no English skills. "I found myself walking the beach, offering to do massages or nails. That's how I learned English."

Now her children attend not one, but two schools: Cambodian classes in the morning and English classes in the afternoon. Her oldest is about to go to university. "All very expensive, so I work every day."

I'm so impressed by her hard work and resilience. It makes me happy that while some people, like that little girl, will probably be stuck in this lifestyle, at least this one woman is using the beach business to elevate her family.

So by buying goods on the beach, did I help or hurt the community as a whole? Are the vendors a nuisance or an important way for locals to make money off of growing tourism? Probably all of those things are true. In a place like Cambodia, things really aren't black and white.

CHAPTER 15.

SOMETIMES TRAVEL SUCKS

There, I said it.

I hit the wall at a guesthouse in Vang Vieng, Laos. One of the party capitals of South East Asia, it's famous for riverbed tubing and riverbank drinking. I had tried to go tubing the day before, but thanks to low water levels and some crooked tuk tuk drivers I got off at the wrong bend in the river and was totally unsuccessful. I didn't really feel like partying anyways. I felt like sitting in my room alone, eating chocolate croissants, and writing. That just seemed like such a waste of time — I could be doing THAT at home.

This was so dumb, I LOVE travel! I'm like a travel evangelist. But I'm sure that even Pat Robertson has an off day. Right then I was just really not feeling it.

I planned this trip for forever. I saved up for two years. TWO YEARS. For two years I lived at home, and worked a boring job and pinned all my motivations, and hopes, and dreams on this adventure. And here I was on this trip, living and breathing it. Close to six months in, and while I had a lot of great stories and photos to share, I'd be lying if I said it has been exactly what I'd hoped it would be. It's rained. A lot. I had some really painful family issues going on at home. And I missed my boyfriend, more than I really should.

Then I reach a place like Vang Vieng. A place that a lot of people adore, but that frankly isn't me. I'm not comfortable there. Hordes of young backpackers day drinking into oblivion and watching *Family Guy* re-runs. Not that I have anything against either of those things, it just did not suit my mood at all. I felt dull. And old.

I was still glad to be traveling, but sometimes I'd look around and think that everyone was having more fun than me. Or that I wasn't t fully taking advantage of the opportunities presented to me. Sometimes, like this day, I just felt really burnt out.

Then I would start to feel terribly guilty. I'm out here, living the dream, living MY dream of writing and working and traveling. Everyone I meet tells me "you're so lucky," and "I wish I could do that." I know I AM lucky, so why am I sitting alone in my room throwing myself a pity party?

I think that when you are traveling long term, it is just impossible to keep up that enthusiasm and adrenaline that you might have on a shorter trip. Day to day living can get you down no matter where you are.

I guess it's probably not supposed to be easy.

One of the most important lessons I think I'll take away from this trip is when to give up. It's hard on my pride, but pushing on when things just aren't right isn't going to get me anywhere but miserable. The second or third time I found myself crying in my guesthouse, alone, I realized something wasn't quite right. I love South East Asia — everything from the friendly people to the beautiful blue beaches to the smiling people. I enjoyed traveling alone and I was doing some of my best writing all trip. I should have been having an awesome time, but for some reason I just**wasn't**.

Describing my symptoms to my dad over G-chat one evening he said very knowingly, "Oh yes, I know what you mean. No more rocks."

You see, when I was 11, my parents bought an RV and took my brother and I on a three-month road trip all over the United States. It was my dad's dream; he'd taken a sabbatical from work, poured over guidebooks and planned an itinerary that included all the great highlights of the American West. It was the trip of a lifetime, which is why he was shocked about two months in when we reached the Badlands, South Dakota and everyone refused to get out of the car.

"What is even here?" my younger brother asked, lazily.

"There are these really beautiful rock forma-"

"We've already seen rocks! Lots of rocks! No more rocks." My dad was dumbfounded. Here we were at one of the most beautiful National Parks in the country and all his kids wanted to do was ride their bikes and maybe go swimming. After two months of non-stop sightseeing we were totally burned out.

It took a little bit longer this time, but I have reached the point of No More Rocks. I was tired. After six months of spending no longer than a week in any given place I was exhausted. It didn't matter how beautiful the scenery was, my brain had reached capacity and all I really wanted was to take a break.

Luckily the cure for No More Rocks syndrome isn't just to give up and go home (at least not always). What was bothering me wasn't the act of being abroad, it was the constantly moving around. The solution then, was simply to stay in one place for a while.

In another life I would have found myself a bar job in Sihanoukville and become a beach bum. As things were I had a far better option. It was time to go back to China.

In the end it's about knowing yourself and your limitations. Sure I could have pressed on for a few more weeks, headed up to Northern Thailand like I'd originally planned. It wouldn't have killed me or anything. But I wouldn't have enjoyed it as much as it deserves to be enjoyed. It wouldn't have been worth it. Thailand will always be there, but I had to do what was best for me — even if it did mean giving up.

CHAPTER 16.

THE TIME I WENT TO A 3D PORNO

Have you heard about the 3-D porno? All of China is abuzz with rumors about Hong Kong's newest movie sensation. Of course it's totally and 100% completely banned behind the Great Firewall, but on opening weekend in Hong Kong it broke records and grossed more than *Avatar*.

Guess what I did on my visa run to Hong Kong?

I've done a lot of activities solo in my day. I have no problem eating at a restaurant alone, going to the beach alone, hell, I even moved to a new city without knowing a single soul, but going to watch a pornographic movie, in a theater no less, all by my lonesome has to be the strangest. I wondered if it would look weird, a lone white girl at a porno on a Sunday night.

Still, everyone is talking about this movie in China and nobody can watch it. Tour companies are even creating organized trips to Hong Kong for people to see The Film. Could I really pass up a bragging opportunity like that? No I could not, so off to the theater I went to see *Sex and Zen: EXTREME Ecstasy*.

Make no mistake: this is a mainstream movie. The theater I went to was also showing *Scream 4*, *Little Red Riding Hood* and whatever that terrible looking movie with Adam Sandler and Jennifer Aniston is. I thought I would feel creepy, but the place was so crowded nobody looked twice at me. The crowd was mostly couples and groups of young people, but some white haired folks were buying popcorn too. Oh and by the way, I was CARDED on my way into the theater. Hopefully by the time I start writing Thirty-Something Travel I will look at least 18.

Once inside the theater I learned that it was apparently BYO3DG (Bring Your Own 3-D Glasses). Really? Is that a thing now? Everyone else seemed prepared, nonchalantly pulling out their personal 3-D spectacles. Luckily I could buy a pair at concessions for $6 Hong Kong.

The nice thing about movie theaters in Asia is you can reserve your seat online. Back in my room I had strategically selected a seat far enough away from other people to not be weird, but on an aisle in case I needed an easy escape. To my consternation I still ended up sitting next to a couple, and had a weirdly tall guy in front of me obscuring the English subtitles.

But you don't need subtitles to look at boobs. Giant, three-dimensional boobs that flopped towards the audience. The film is an adaptation of a classical Chinese novel, *The Carnal Prayer Mat*, written in 1657, which totally makes sense because everyone knows that old books are the dirtiest. It follows a young scholar as he abandons his wife and descends into an underworld of sex and violence. The first half started off well enough — kind of a slapstick comedy with some sex thrown in. The main character bumbles along in his quest to become a sex god, with many jokes centering around his tiny manhood and lack of stamina. At one point he has his penis surgically removed and replaced with that of a donkey. Crude yes, but also kind of hilarious and the audience was roaring with laughter.

By the way, the term "porno" is being used fairly loosely here. I'm no expert, but this film definitely falls on the "soft core" side of the spectrum. While there's a great deal of female nudity and some very shrill fake orgasms, the movie is definitely devoid of any explicit hard core sex. Considering the cast is made up of mainstream Hong Kong actors (with a few Japanese AV starts thrown in for good measure), the chances of actually seeing two people have real sex were pretty low.

Right when the movie had lulled me in with its raunchy humor, the second hour took a dark turn. A REALLY dark turn. Several people who we've come to identify with (male and female) are violently raped or murdered. One girl is literally, umm, bonked to *death*. This isn't done in a funny way, granted it's pretty hard to rape someone humorously. During one weird sexual torture scene I almost walked out of the theater. This movie wasn't fun anymore, it was just... disturbing.

SPOILER ALERT: In the end the now-castrated hero and his long-lost wife (who has been tortured, raped repeatedly then locked inside a chastity belt), do get to live happily ever after. They've learned that you don't need to have sex to be in love. Seriously. This is the moral of the world's first 3-D erotic film. Basically, it was the world's longest, most explicit abstinence PSA.

I left the theater feeling pretty bewildered. I'm not really sure what to make of this movie or its incredible popularity. Is this what gets people off in Hong Kong? On the one hand the novelty of watching people get it on in three dimensions is kind of cool. On the other…. ugh. What should have been novel and harmless fun ended up being pretty unpleasant.

Considering the runaway success of this movie though, I'm pretty sure you can expect to see 3-D pornography popping up at a theater near you. Just remember to bring your own 3-D glasses; I don't think you're going to want to touch the used ones.

CHAPTER 17.

HOW I WAS WRONG

I always knew I wanted to travel, and amazingly I never really wavered in that belief. I was so excited and so proud. When I got on that plane to Tokyo in September 2010 I thought I had it all figured out. I was so wrong.

In the course of this project I've had to go back and look at a lot of the old posts I wrote before I quit my job. Back when long-term travel was just a dream, a golden goal. It's pretty amazing to see how WRONG I was about my own way of traveling.

Here are some of the major things I mistakenly believed:

That I Would Stick To My Itinerary

This trip I planned only vaguely resembles the trip that actually happened. I never made it to New Zealand, or Egypt or Eastern Europe. I never hiked Hadrian's Wall with my Dad. I actually never even made it all the way around the world, so my entire trip was totally mis-named.

I'd still love to do all of those things at some point but even though I didn't check all the boxes, I ended up having entirely unexpected adventures. I never would have dreamed that I'd spend three months living in China of all places, or that I'd fall in love with Vietnam, or make multiple trips to Hong Kong and Macau. Or that instead of going home and getting a job I'd end up going on to backpack through South America with my boyfriend (THAT is a whole other book). These things were nowhere on my radar when I wrote down my plans two years ago.

This is a big part of why I now always tell people to be as flexible as possible with your big trip plans. I could never have anticipated 75% of the things that have happened in the past few years and I'm so grateful that my plans were loose enough to be changed (and that I didn't buy a RTW ticket).

That I Would Travel Alone Forever

I obviously put my foot in my mouth on this one: in the year before I left I made a pretty big deal about traveling the world ALONE. I wasn't waiting around for any guy to show up! Solo travel forever! Well, I still love solo travel and I'll never really give it up completely, but like I said above, the plan changed. The resulting relationship totally scrambled my itinerary, my travel style, everything. It was the start of an adventure that's ongoing to this day.

When you're traveling for a long time and totally uprooting your life, you have to be ready to adapt to the curve balls life will almost certainly throw at you. I'm just glad I didn't pass up on one of the most terrific things in my life because I was too rigid in my thinking.

That I Would Get Rid Of All My Stuff

When you read a lot of travel blogs, you start to recognize the same patterns and process everyone goes through when gearing up to travel. The money-saving, plane-ticket buying, life re-ordering stuff. One of the big components that comes up again and again is the idea of selling all, or at least most of your possessions. In addition to raising money for your trip I think it's supposed to be a life cleansing process or something.

I bought way into that. I was so ready to sell all my crap and travel the world with a clean slate, I even wrote an article about it. Well, guess what, it didn't happen. I donated a huge truckload of clothes to Goodwill, I sold my car, but that was it. Selling stuff was too time consuming both physically and emotionally. I left behind three bookcases of books, a closet of clothing, a tiny stuffed animal collection and more.

You know what? I'm glad I did, because I'm back now and that winter clothing came in handy after all. You're free to pick and choose which advice you want to take, and you don't have to fit your trip into anyone else's mold. Just do what makes sense.

That I Am An Organized Person

My intentions were good. When I was planning my trip I had spreadsheets and word documents, all meticulously researched. I had budgets mapped out and timetables. Everything was planned and perfect.

Of course, once I got on the road I ignored it all. Never looked at any of it. I estimated my budget based on the amount in my bank account and frantically Googled each new city when I arrived. Because that is just the way that I work. It was fine, I didn't run out of money, I only got lost once a day and I still saw a lot of awesome stuff.

What I failed to realize is that traveling was not going to somehow magically transform me into the awesome Type A person I so badly want to be. All my bad habits from home were still my bad habits on the road. I wish I had realized that earlier and planned a system that would actually work for me.

That I Would Take My Malaria Pills

I carried around 300 capsules of doxycycline for months, just waiting til I got to Laos to crack those bad boys open. I took them for a week before I had to stop. They made me so nauseous all the time! I decided to make do with extra strength bug spray instead.

Now, I'm **not** saying you shouldn't take your malaria pills. Getting malaria would suck. It's just that once I was on the ground in SE Asia I was able to assess the situation more carefully than I could from 1000 miles away and make the best decision for myself.

That I Knew Anything At All

I look back on myself three years ago and I think wow, what business did she have starting a travel blog, giving other people advice on how to travel?

So many things didn't work out the way I planned them at all, but I don't feel bad about a second of it. I couldn't have known how the reality of the road would match up to my expectations, and neither can you, because everyone is as unique as the trips they plan. That's part of the adventure I guess.

CHAPTER 18.

A YEAR WITHOUT MAKE-UP

In a past life, I used to wear a lot of make-up.

Actually, that's not accurate. I know girls who wear a lot of make-up — girls who practically paint on a new face each day. I was never a girl who wore her appearance as a disguise. My daily routine was along the lines of moisturizer, powder foundation, eye shadow, curler, mascara and maybe some blush or lip gloss.

When you consider the thousands of beauty products out there this is not really all that much. Still, after two years of traveling it's absurd to me that I went through all of that every single morning for years and years. What a lot of time and effort! I could have been sleeping!

When I started living on the road I pretty much quit wearing make-up cold turkey. I had packed the basics (including my eyelash curler — don't judge!), but I immediately stopped using it. At first I was too jetlagged to bother, then there didn't seem to be a point. It was just more trouble than it was worth.

In Australia we lived out of a van: the idea of putting on mascara in the rearview mirror was almost comical. In South East Asia it would have immediately melted off anyways. In China I already looked so radically different from everyone else on campus I just couldn't see any point in trying to dress things up. All of a sudden six months had gone by and I'd worn make-up maybe two or three times. You know, for big nights out.

I sure didn't miss it. In fact I abandoned most of my beauty routines from home: my hair was in a constant ponytail and I'd lost all qualms about wearing the same dress four days in a row. It wasn't that I didn't care about my appearance; it was that suddenly, for the first time since I hit puberty, **my own face just seemed like enough**. I didn't need to add anything to make myself presentable to the world.

Oddly, even during my three months in Argentina, where women at the grocery store are made up to the nines, I just couldn't be bothered. I wasn't like those women, I never would be, so what was the point? I was an outsider, exempt from their beauty rules, and it was really freeing.

In my past life I remember being late to work one day and forgetting to apply any make-up. All day people were asking me if I was sick. This didn't happen when I travelled. Nobody commented on my bare face and Mike still seemed to think I was pretty hot. In pictures I may not look like a model, but I don't look half bad. My beauty secret was written all over my face: I looked so, so happy. Smiling eyes totally make up for a lack of eyeliner.

You can look at this two ways: either I was so content with my life I didn't feel like I needed cover-up, OR realizing I didn't need a half hour of primping each morning to look like a decent human being made me super happy. Either way, it sure does make our cultural beauty mores seem like some major oppressive bullshit.

This realization was compounded by my anthropological observation of the lengths women go all around the world to fit the cultural concept of beauty. The Barbie-like women in Japan, teetering in high heels and fake eyelashes. The skin-bleaching creams for sale at the supermarket in China. The absolutely incredible architectural marvel of fake boobs and butts in Colombia. We're all suffering for beauty — it just seems sillier when it's not your own culture pressing in.

I'd like to say the moral is that make-up is totally useless and I never wear it now. This would be a lie. A kind of judgmental lie. Now that I'm back in the US, certain beauty routines have crept back in. It's vanity through and through: I can not go out for drinks with my beautiful girlfriends and be the one washed out weirdo — I just can't, the beauty ideals here are just too strong and I'm not immune to their power.

I definitely don't wear make-up every day — certainly not around the house or out to the store. I'm still a low maintenance girl, I always have been: I don't wear heels, I bite my nails, my two hair style choices are basically "up" or "down." But, I just bought a huge load of sparkly make-up from Ulta, and I'm currently obsessing over finding the perfect wedding dress.

It's complicated of course. What travel has taught me though is that it's okay to pick and choose what cultural beauty standards I want to participate in. And not to buy into the idea that they are laws or even rules. Because they ARE totally arbitrary — unique to our culture and space and time. It wasn't until I spent some time opting out that I realized there was something to **opt out of**. It's the choice that makes it liberating.

WHY YOUR TWENTIES ARE TERRIBLE/AWESOME

I flew home in June of 2011. I wasn't there long before I was preparing for my next major backpacking trip, this one consisting of nine months in South America. Since then I've been almost constantly on the move, never in one place for too long. I've discovered that travel isn't just something you can "get out of your system," it's more like an addiction that grows and grows.

When I was 21 years old my mother told me that her twenties were the hardest decade of her life. This kind of puzzled me at the time. After all — I'd just gotten the ability to drink legally; my life was going great! I was getting ready to graduate from college, my world was full of friends and endless possibilities. If this was what the twenties decade of my life was about, I thought I would be okay.

Now, in my late twenties I'm a bit more circumspect. Every year so far has felt like a lifetime: an individual universe of life lessons, future defining decisions and self-contemplation. There's been a lot of fun parts and a lot of intense parts but the takeaway is that man, being in my twenties is exhausting.

Our twenties is when most of us make the major life decisions that are going to affect the rest of our years: what kind of person will you be? What will you do for work? Will you get married, and to who? There's a lot of pressure to choose wisely, to choose as if our lives depended on it. And that is a bitch, because there is just no way to know if you are making the right choice until maybe even years later.

In a way, this is what makes leading a typical, traditional lifestyle so appealing. There is a certain comfort in following the status quo: so many people can't all be wrong, right? If you do what everybody else is doing your life might not be very spontaneous, but at least you'll feel secure. You'll know what comes next because it's all been done before, a million times, by everyone else.

For some people though, the typical American lifestyle just doesn't cut it. They want something else, something different, and that in itself is pretty scary. Breaking away from what's normal can be absolutely terrifying (and exciting) because there is just no way of knowing how it will pay off. It's higher risk, and hopefully higher reward.

Despite what my own experiences were, I don't really care if people quit their job to go travel, or just take one-week vacations whenever they get the chance. It doesn't matter how long or on what scale, the point is to seek out the world.

It's not a better choice, or a worse one, but either way it's pretty scary to be in your twenties and trying to be the architect of your destiny. When the doubts creep in there's only one thing I know how to do. I take a deep breath and I wait it out. Because even if the doubts don't totally recede the panic does. Then I can actually think clearly about what I'm doing with my life.

I also remind myself that nobody else has it figured out either. Life's not a race, it's an evolution. It's growing and changing and while that's uncomfortable and leads to late night wine and tears, it's normal, even preferable.

That's the thing right? While your twenties are tough and emotionally exhausting, they are also pretty intense, fun and awesome. That's the reason

I'm so keen on people traveling in their twenties. It's such an intense time, when you learn so much about yourself, and travel just accelerates the process.

And that's what I wanted you to know.

ABOUT THE AUTHOR

Stephanie Yoder is a girl who can't sit still! Since graduating from college in 2007, she has been either traveling or planning to travel. In the past six years she's lived on four continents and traveled everywhere from the Great Wall of China to the Great Barrier Reef. She's now a full time blogger and travel writer who chronicles her adventures across the globe on www.twenty-somethingtravel.com.